CHILDREN'S STORYTELLERS

Nikki Grimes

by Chris Bowman

BLASTOFF! READERS

BELLWETHER MEDIA • MINNEAPOLIS, MN

Note to Librarians, Teachers, and Parents:

Blastoff! Readers are carefully developed by literacy experts and combine standards-based content with developmentally appropriate text.

Level 1 provides the most support through repetition of high-frequency words, light text, predictable sentence patterns, and strong visual support.

Level 2 offers early readers a bit more challenge through varied simple sentences, increased text load, and less repetition of high-frequency words.

Level 3 advances early-fluent readers toward fluency through increased text and concept load, less reliance on visuals, longer sentences, and more literary language.

Level 4 builds reading stamina by providing more text per page, increased use of punctuation, greater variation in sentence patterns, and increasingly challenging vocabulary.

Level 5 encourages children to move from "learning to read" to "reading to learn" by providing even more text, varied writing styles, and less familiar topics.

Whichever book is right for your reader, Blastoff! Readers are the perfect books to build confidence and encourage a love of reading that will last a lifetime!

This edition first published in 2018 by Bellwether Media, Inc.

No part of this publication may be reproduced in whole or in part without written permission of the publisher. For information regarding permission, write to Bellwether Media, Inc., Attention: Permissions Department, 5357 Penn Avenue South, Minneapolis, MN 55419.

Library of Congress Cataloging-in-Publication Data
Names: Bowman, Chris, 1990- author.
Title: Nikki Grimes / by Chris Bowman.
Description: Minneapolis, MN : Bellwether Media, Inc., 2018. | Series: Blastoff! Readers: Children's Storytellers | Includes bibliographical references and index. | Audience: Grades 2-5
Identifiers: LCCN 2016055077 (print) | LCCN 2017013267 (ebook) | ISBN 9781626176508 (hardcover : alk. paper) | ISBN 9781681033808 (ebook)
Subjects: LCSH: Grimes, Nikki–Juvenile literature. | Poets, American–20th century–Biography–Juvenile literature. | African American women poets–Biography–Juvenile literature.
Classification: LCC PS3557.R489982 (ebook) | LCC PS3557.R489982 Z56 2018 (print) | DDC 811/.54 [B] –dc23
LC record available at https://lccn.loc.gov/2016055077

Text copyright © 2018 by Bellwether Media, Inc. Blastoff! Readers and associated logos are trademarks and/or registered trademarks of Bellwether Media, Inc. SCHOLASTIC, CHILDREN'S PRESS, and associated logos are trademarks and/or registered trademarks of Scholastic Inc.

Editor: Betsy Rathburn   Designer: Josh Brink

Printed in the United States of America, North Mankato, MN.

Table of Contents

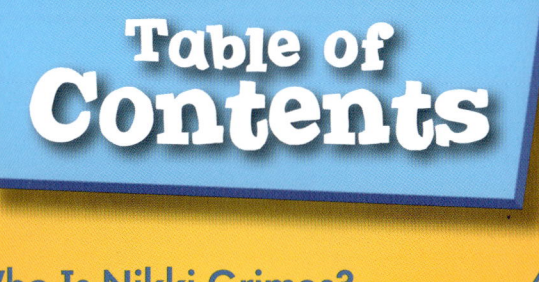

Who Is Nikki Grimes? 4
Something on Her Mind 6
Growin' Up 10
The Road to Being Published 14
Nikki's Notebook 16
Giving Words Wings 20
Glossary 22
To Learn More 23
Index 24

Who Is Nikki Grimes?

Nikki Grimes is a best-selling author for children, teens, and adults. Readers connect with her **fiction** and poetry for its honest look at the struggles of growing up.

"Poetry is just natural for children. It's part of their lives!"
— Nikki Grimes

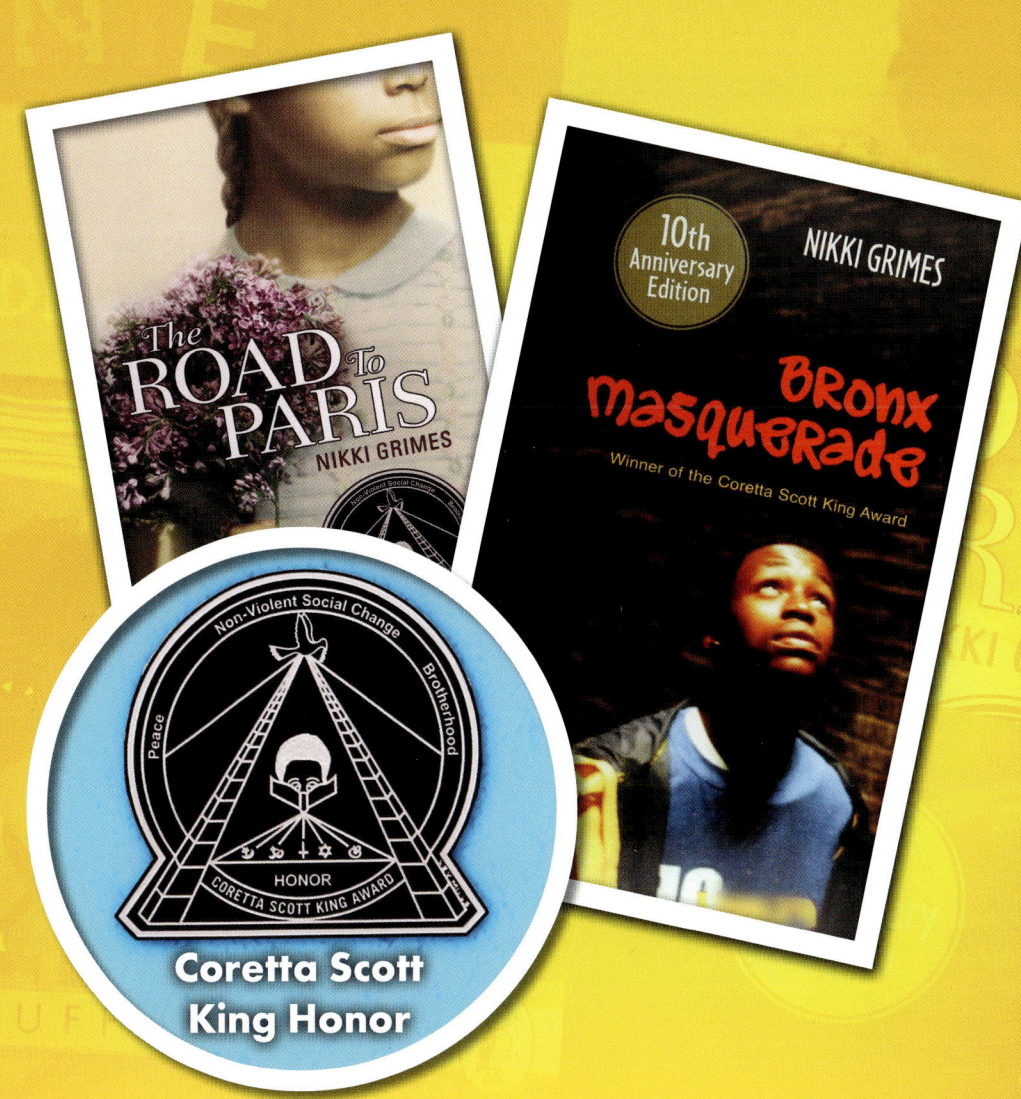

Coretta Scott King Honor

Nikki's books have won many awards. Her popular **novel** Bronx Masquerade won the **Coretta Scott King Award**. Five of her other books received Coretta Scott King Honors.

Something on Her Mind

Nikki was born on October 20, 1950, in New York City, New York. She had an older sister, Carol.

"Reading and writing were my survival tools when I was a kid."
Nikki Grimes

New York City, New York

Nikki's parents had a troubled marriage. Nikki and Carol often stayed in other homes when their parents fought. When Nikki was 5 years old, her parents separated.

After their parents separated, Nikki and Carol were sent to different **foster homes**. Nikki found a home with a family in Ossining, New York. There, she fell in love with words. Nikki wrote her first poem at age 6.

Nikki also liked reading. But she rarely felt connected to the stories. Few were written about African-American children like her.

"As you push out from the center of that world and explore worlds beyond, your sense of what is possible for your own life grows."
Nikki Grimes

Growin' Up

When Nikki was 10 years old, her mother remarried. Then Nikki moved back home. But life was still difficult for the family. They lived in a dangerous neighborhood.

Nikki never stopped writing. She decided to write stories for kids like her when she grew up. When she was 13 years old, Nikki gave her first poetry reading.

fun fact
Growing up, Nikki enjoyed swimming, running, and playing basketball.

Nikki was a good student in school. But she struggled after her father passed away. One of her high school English teachers helped her handle the loss.

James Baldwin

fun fact

When she was growing up, Nikki met the author James Baldwin. He helped her develop her writing skills.

Rutgers University

After high school, Nikki joined a writing group. She went to college a few years later. Nikki studied English **literature** and African languages at Rutgers University.

The Road to Being Published

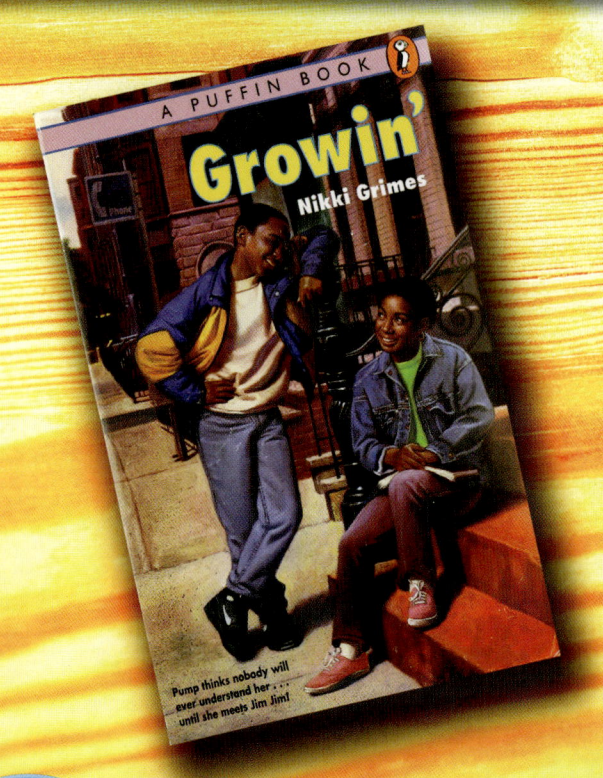

fun fact
One of Nikki's radio jobs was in Sweden. She lived there for six years!

After graduating, Nikki studied in Tanzania. Then she worked in radio and photography. She also held jobs in libraries and as an editor. Meanwhile, she continued to write.

Nikki's first children's book, *Growin'*, was **published** in 1977. The next year, her first poetry book for children came out. By 1991, she was focused on writing full-time.

SELECTED WORKS

Meet Danitra Brown (1994)

Jazmin's Notebook (1998)

Bronx Masquerade (2002)

Talkin' About Bessie (2002)

Dark Sons (2005)

The Road to Paris (2006)

Barack Obama: Son of Promise, Child of Hope (2008)

Words with Wings (2013)

Garvey's Choice (2016)

One Last Word: Wisdom from the Harlem Renaissance (2017)

Nikki's Notebook

Nikki's writing often explores relationships between friends, families, and communities. She uses poetry to **encourage** kids to chase their dreams.

"I'm looking to give voice to…children who aren't able to find themselves in the books they read."
Nikki Grimes

Nikki writes for readers who might not **relate** to other children's books. Her stories are usually about African-American children facing big challenges.

Nikki's stories also teach understanding. Sometimes people act differently when they are sad or upset. Nikki's stories help readers learn to see people in new ways.

POP CULTURE CONNECTION

In 2008, Nikki wrote *Barack Obama: Son of Promise, Child of Hope* months before Barack Obama became the first African-American President of the United States. She combined poetry with pictures to tell the story of the 44th president.

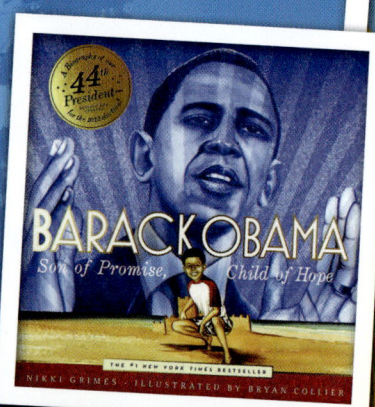

"Writing is something you can just do for yourself."
Nikki Grimes

18

Nikki often writes about pain and loss. She knows that many kids struggle with tough problems. She wants them to feel like they are not alone.

Giving Words Wings

Nikki has written more than 45 books in her long **career**. But she shows no sign of slowing down. Nikki still works six days per week!

"Where is a safer place to learn about another culture than between the pages of a book?"
Nikki Grimes

IMPORTANT DATES

1950: Nikki is born on October 20.

1977: Nikki's first children's book, *Growin'*, is published.

1978: *Something on My Mind,* Nikki's first book of poetry, comes out.

2003: Nikki is given the Coretta Scott King Award for *Bronx Masquerade*.

2005: Nikki receives the Southern California Children's Book Association Golden Dolphin Award for her body of work.

2005: *What is Goodbye?* is named an ALA Notable Book.

2006: The National Council of Teachers of English Award for Excellence in Poetry for Children is given to Nikki.

2007: The Coretta Scott King Honor is given to Nikki for *The Road to Paris*.

2009: *Barack Obama: Son of Promise, Child of Hope* receives the NAACP Image Award for Outstanding Literary Work.

2016: Nikki receives the Virginia Hamilton Literary Award.

No matter what her next project is, Nikki continues to create characters people can relate to. Her stories and poems give a voice to readers of all ages!

Glossary

career—a job someone does for a long time

Coretta Scott King Award—an award given each year to the best African-American authors and illustrators of books for children and young adults; the Coretta Scott King Award is given to first place and the Coretta Scott King Honors are given to the runners-up.

encourage—to give hope or confidence

fiction—written stories about people and events that are not real

foster homes—houses in which children are cared for by adults other than their parents

literature—written works, often books, that are highly respected

novel—a longer written story, usually about made-up characters and events

published—printed for a public audience

relate—to connect with and understand

To Learn More

AT THE LIBRARY
Bowman, Chris. *Christopher Paul Curtis*. Minneapolis, Minn.: Bellwether Media, 2017.

Grimes, Nikki. *Bronx Masquerade*. New York, N.Y.: Dial Books, 2002.

Wheeler, Jill C. *Nikki Grimes*. Edina, Minn.: ABDO Pub., 2011.

ON THE WEB
Learning more about Nikki Grimes is as easy as 1, 2, 3.

1. Go to www.factsurfer.com.

2. Enter "Nikki Grimes" into the search box.

3. Click the "Surf" button and you will see a list of related web sites.

With factsurfer.com, finding more information is just a click away.

Index

awards, 5
Baldwin, James, 12
Barack Obama: Son of Promise, Child of Hope, 18
Bronx Masquerade, 5
Carol (sister), 6, 7, 9
childhood, 6, 7, 9, 10, 12
Coretta Scott King Award, 5
education, 12, 13, 14
family, 6, 7, 9, 10, 12
foster homes, 9
Growin', 15
important dates, 21
jobs, 14
New York City, 6
Ossining, New York, 9
poetry, 4, 9, 10, 15, 16, 21
pop culture connection, 18
quotes, 4, 6, 9, 16, 18, 20
Rutgers University, 13
selected works, 15
Tanzania, 14
themes, 4, 16, 17, 18, 19
writing, 9, 10, 12, 13, 14, 15, 16, 19

The images in this book are reproduced through the courtesy of: Picture Perfect/ Shutterstock/ Rex Features, front cover, p. 8; Josh Brink, front cover (books), pp. 5 (left, right, bottom), 14, 18; John Shearer/ Getty Images, p. 4; Ilya Dreyvitser/ Getty Images, pp. 7, 11; Sueddeutsche Zeitung Photo/ Alamy, p. 12; DenisTangneyJr, p. 13; Frederick M. Brown/ Stringer, pp. 16, 20; Wavebreakmedia, p. 17; Africa Studio, p. 19.